A Love Supreme

A Love Supreme

Professor Arturo

NYQ Books™

The New York Quarterly Foundation, Inc.
New York, New York

NYQ Books™ is an imprint of The New York Quarterly Foundation, Inc.

The New York Quarterly Foundation, Inc.
P. O. Box 2015
Old Chelsea Station
New York, NY 10113

www.nyq.org

First Edition

Set in New Baskerville

Layout by Raymond P. Hammond

Cover Photograph by Professor Arturo

Author Photo by David Lotus

Library of Congress Control Number: 2016941106

ISBN: 978-1-63045-032-8

A Love Supreme

Acknowledgements

Maple Leaf Rag V, Portals Press, 2014:
"Second Line (to Jayne Cortez and Amiri Baraka)"

NOLA Diaspora:
"Fake," "Motto," and "The Life, Loves and Legend of Marie Laveau"

Contents

for the lovers and the haters

A Love Supreme

Acknowledgment

My heart is not still troubled
    for I rejoice in the knowledge of You...
Your perfection and power inhabit all creation
You are infinite beginnings and worlds without end
You are reawakening and resurgence
Blessed are those who hear Your voice
Blessed are those who truly walk in the Spirit
Blessed are those who are cast from the template of Your care
Blessed are those who stumble and stagger without knowledge of You
    for their doom and destruction are ever imminent...
Your children are treated as chattel
The deep roots of their sins infect their descendants
Their curses and cries are everywhere about me
Their transgressions abide in the spawning of generations
They hear not Your voice, nor heed Your word
They feel not Your goodness and nourishment encircling their pitiful flesh
Their environs are the dwelling of folly and asses
I have pursued the advice of fools
I have sought the perfumed pleasures of harlots
I have seen their abominations and scandalous lives
You summoned my endowments, but I heeded You not
I write these words so that the unborn can take heed from my recklessness
    for the things of the world are impermanent and wretched
The knowledge of Your compassion is aflame in the marrow of my mind
    for all things are in Your plan
        all power is in Your hand
All ascendancy is in Your glory
All truth is in Your story...

Amen...

Sunday, January 5, 2014 10:50 AM
Stamford, CT

Resolution

Father,
Today, in this first day of the earthlings' new year
I resolve to bathe forever in Your rivers of living water
where I will believe in You and never thirst
for You are the bread of life in spirit and truth…
I have been in this world for a while
(and You know where I have been)
I have dwelt among the sinners and saints
drunk wine with the wicked and supped with the corrupt
I implore Your forgiveness and seek Your blessings
for I am but flesh and bone…
If not for the Comforter
If not for Your Spirit
my corporeal demise might have long been assured…
I worship in faith's garden
and feel these words reaching heavenward…
I am Your unswerving servant for time without end
I am the voice that You inspire inside this insubstantial embodiment
I am Your creation, however imperfect
for You are the impassioned voice that inspires and inflames…
You are a love poem to the loveless
You are safe harbor to the spurned
You are all conception and creation
You are endless thought and virtuosity
for it is Your radiance that shimmers in the seams of my soul …
The skies and the seas are Yours
The mountains and the pebbles are Yours
All encompassment and creation are Yours
All reverence and veneration are Yours
I will sing Your glory beyond the day of days
and dance through the dawning of the fineness of our futures
until we reside in the transcendence of Your house forever

Amen…

Wednesday, January 1, 2014 9:07 AM
Stamford, CT

16

Pursuance

Father,
Anoint these words with Your spirit
so that my heart can express Your truth…
Blessed be all creation for Her power of birth
Blessed be Your salvation to believers in You
-the all-Powerful Musician of Life
-Holy of all Holies
-mercy to the merciless
-the greatest glory conceivable…
You brought the mother of all winds to cleanse my heart and clear my path
(Who but the sinner can speak of sin with authority?)
I called out in the night and You answered
You took my hand and guided me from the storm
-grasped me firmly amidst the shadows and pulled me to enlightenment
-saved me from the embittered of the earth…
Their perception is limited
The pungent fruits of their pitiable harvest are but an impermanent passing
Did they not know the consequences of their folly?
Could not Your power pierce their secret selves?
I strayed from Your words and Your path of light
I supped with sinners and feasted with transgressors
I drank with devourers and frequented ungodly seducers
My head strained heavenward, but my heart still dwelled on the earth
You bore witness to my depravity and guided me to love again
I exalt and praise Your name
I give thanks for Your wonders
(for Your miracle of life still courses through this embodiment)
I have no fear, want, or trembling
    for Your goodness envelops and encompasses me
No longer will I stray from Your fount of inspiration
    and I will forever worship and praise You more abundantly…

Amen…

Friday, July 18, 2014 9:34 PM
Stamford, CT

17

Psalm

I come to You in Your name and plead for Your mercy
I sing to Your glory and the strength of the truthful tongue
I sing a song of Your salvation and the bright light You bring
I celebrate Your majesty and proclaim Your largess
I offer oblation to heaven's perpetual light...
You know my heart and the inner man
Your loving kindness guides my every breath
You protect me and keep me from all harm
I dwell safely in Your reassurance
All nature is testament to Your mastery
You shepherd me from the ungodly
    and I am shielded from the world's wicked spirits...
The power of Your spoken word expresses Your eternal eminence
The days of this life are near-at-hand
Destruction and desolation are imminent
I walk in Your name and judiciousness
You know my yesterday thoughts and tomorrow dreams
You are the Revealer of all truth
-the Healer of all afflictions
-all imagination and thought
I delight in Your knowledge and welcome Your protection
Your life force overflows with strength and certainty
May Your song be forever sung
    throughout the worlds You brought into being...

Amen...

Friday, July 18, 2014 10:44 PM
Stamford, CT

Supplication

Second Line

(to Jayne Cortez and Amiri Baraka)

I
Dirge

Death's door opens...
We are bereaved indeed
when perchance a soul whom we encountered leaves
-just as certain as we all must
face our destiny and return to dust

And in the midst of such despair
when mournful departure permeates the air
we ask ourselves of the whys and whens
of the stillness and their silent pens...

Though chance or choice might play a part
in our lives and loves and art
we are here but for a second's pace
in lieu of time and unbounded space

Their words have healed and steered the way
in our screams and dreams throughout the day
to guide us forward in the night
and enfold us with unearthly light

In risqué verse or genteel rhyme
where life is such a crucial climb
We rise to heights from these poets' hearts
from the faraway gates of their shrouded parts

We wail and mourn and shed our tears
and revamp our hopes for future years
their vision endures to soothe our sadness
from a celestial fount of eternal gladness

We howl and yowl and question why
such blessed essence should bid goodbye
But prideful death just cannot smile
because the poets trod that further mile
for the future holds we know not what
when death's door closes so abruptly shut...

II
Dance

To the poets...
to the weavers of words and makers of rhyme
(word warriors)
to the jazz poets and the jizz poets
(battenin' down the hatches and waterin' the cannon)
for the poets
for the scribes
the vernal fire-spitters and Ancient-Agers
(Blessed be their hearts and jingly parts)
to the tone and tenor of their universe
(from the people, to the people, for the people)
for the poets...
for the poets of the people
(Where they at-where they at-where they at?)
Poets just in from the rain
Poets from the storm
Poets from the Ninth Ward (doing a heck of a job)
Poets from Poughkeepsie
Poets from Ma-ha'-in'
Poets who be hay-in' (No he di-'in'...)
Poets who be abomination to all creation
Poets who mouthspout "Yes we can"
-change we can believe in (chump change)
Poets with Ph.D.'s
Poets that be sittin' 'round sayin' stuff like "WORD...WORD UP..."
Poets who be sayin' "Habari Gani...OOGA BOOGA...Where y'at?!..."

Poets with exotic-sounding African and Islamic names (who still act
    like kneegroes)
Poets who believe everything they're taught
Poets who play it like they so intellectually astute (and they just as
    ign'ant as me)
Poets that talk about knowns and unknowns and the things that they
    knew that they knew (which were the known unknowns) which
    is to say that there were things that they knew they didn't know.
    But there were also unknown unknowns that they didn't know they
    didn't know (DUH-UH-UH-uh-uh-uh...)
Poets who sing the praises of the beautiful black women in Nation Time
    (cliché)
Poets on Open Mic Night: My Nubian Ki-i-i-i-i-ing...
    My Nubian Quee-ee-ee-een...(cliché)
Poets who be red, black and blue in green all by themselves
    in the heat of the night (cliché)
the poets of our blood, blood (with some exceptions)
Poets where dead lecturers live who rise, rise and raise rays
to the political poets and the greeting card poets (*Tender is the night...*)
Academic poets   polemic poets
to those polished and proper pundits and punsters
-the unholy grail of their shallow solutions (and rudimentary renditions)
to the poets at the readings who always goin' overtime and bogartin' the mic
(Oops! My ba-a-a-a-a-a-ad)
To the poets around us, within us, and us in them (the people's poets)
Poets in the tradition:
        "I got ba-na-nas, watermell-on, sweet pato-oo-oo-oo-oo-tee!
        I got ba-na-nas, watermell-on rade to dee rind! –so goo-oo-oo–
        ood it keep the ba-a-a-a-a-aby from cryin'...!"
Poets like Aunt Sweet and Momma Rachel: "The Lawd don't like ugly...
Everybody happy on weddin' day...Take one to know one...take care'
be better than 'beg pardon'...Don't rock the boat—'specially when you
sittin' in it...Some folks don't know what's good 'til it's gone...If they
wasn't no losin' they couldn't be no winnin'... A hard haid make a soft
behind...Keep on doin' what you doin'; keep gittin' what you gittin'...
It ain't what people call you; it's what you answer to...The dog that bring

tail—take tale…Some days you the pigeon; some days you the statue…Show me who you hang with and I'll show you what you is…Don't let yo' right hand know what yo' left hand doin'…Don't throw away the baby with the bathwater…Figures don't lie, but liars figure…Ign'ance is its own reward…Don't shoot all the dogs 'cause one of 'em got fleas…Never give a white man all yo' money…Every goodbye ain't gone…You find yo' bottom when you stop diggin'…Don't pray too hard for what you want—you just might git it…Don't put all yo' eggs in one basket…White meat don't eat white meat…When you lays down with dogs you gits fleas…Never compare yo' insides to somebody else's outsides…Father don't always know best – 'less he Father Time…If you wanta see a rainbow you gotta put up with a lil' rain…Just 'cuz yo' shoes is polished don't mean you ain't got no holes in the sole…Now git out my face boy…I gots washin' to do…"

-DEM kinda poets, pirates, prophets, and partners…
-liberation's libation to future generations
    from the edge of death's highway (the road we all must travel)
Blessed be those who harken to the tragedies and triumphs of their brief breadth of life
as we bury our dead, wipe away our tears
and continue the memory of their sacrifice in our struggle…

Tuesday, Feb. 4, 2014 10:51 PM
Stamford, CT

The Life, Loves and Legend of Marie Laveau

(September 10, 1801 – June 16, 1881)

Some say she came from heaven (some say from down below)
but I'ma give the four-eleven 'bout Marie Laveau...

From Baton Rouge to Baltimore they all knew her name
From the swamplands to the boardrooms they whispered of her fame

She burned exotic incense and wore the prettiest shiny pearls
She was the envy of the wimmins and the idol of the girls

Her head was wrapped in scarlet; her lips were like red wine
Her eyes outshined the stars 'cause the girl was just so fine

She was sweet like cherry chocolates and tasted like caramel candies
with golden velvet skin (that dazzled the tomcat dandies)

She knew so many secrets that put the match to flame
and had a beauty so rare—put Cleopatra to shame

She made 'Lisbeth look like Twiggy and Marilyn look like Moe
Such a dark, comely beauty was Marie Laveau...

She was a pure pound o' flesh (not one wasted ounce)
She was big where it mattered (and small where it counts)

The gentlemen would smile and the ladies would frown
whenever that fine, brown woman chanced to come around

When she walked down the street every male head would turn
All the girlfriends and wives would do a sizzlin' burn

She'd make a strong man weak, a wise man dumb
-make a quick man slow, make a goin' man come

She was exotic, hypnotic, an intoxicating beauty
She took Jean Lafitte's big barrel o' booty

She hung out with a cat named Jiminy Cricket
and sang in the midnight hour with the Wicked Pickett

She knew Pussycat Nell, the harlot from hell
(You might notta met her, but you'd know the smell)

She knew Frisco Jenny and Way Out Willy,
Cherokee Bill, and a kid named Billy

She knew Typhoid Mary and Sioux City Sue, Pussy Galore and Cat Ballou,
Boston Blackie and Alvarez Kelly, Sugarmouth Sam and a Bly named "Nelly"

She was a right queenly woman and was impeccably clean
She was a real fancy woman—make a old man dream

make a young man holler—make a sad man laugh
She took the Parish Sheriff's rod (and his deputy's staff)

The mens all loved her and they'd spend every dime
They'd go away broke (but they'd come every time)

She knew Amelia Bedilia and Montana Belle
-hung with old Slim Greer on his way down to hell

She was in the kitchen with Dinah, in the Gulf with Katrina
The mens would woo her and wine her whenever they seen her

She knew Rattlesnake Dick and Foo Manchu,
  Big Harold Parker and Mr. Magoo

She was a real fine dresser (wasn't no slob)
She'd lock the bedroom door and turn that knob

She made the Thin Man fat, the Tall Man short
She made the vejjitibble man give up his horse and his cart

She was sassy and spicy (like yo' momma' dirty rice)
She'd take the flame outa fire and put yo' soul on ice

She knew Filthy McNasty and Iron Chest Charlie
She cut rugs with Astaire, made music with Marley

She danced by the waters with the spirits and saints
with such pleasure and passion (weren't no complaints)

On St. John's Eve she'd strut and sway all night
And in Congo Square she would shake up a sight

Dynamite Dick was her very best friend
She might even squeeze a cherry every now and then

She'd visit Parish Prison and bring the inmates some cookin'
They'd start up a riot (she was so good-lookin')

They'd didn't mess with her 'cause she was so boss
All the inmates and the warden wanted summa her sauce

She fixed that red gravy that made the mens love her
It took 69 nights for them to recover

Her potions and tonics would heal anything—
run away the Winter and bring back the Spring

She was the Queen of New Orleans (both slave and free)
and beloved by all despite her pedigree

She'd conjure up memories from way 'cross the seas
cure the hottest fever with a cool, calming breeze

She tried to end executions in the Congo Square
-didn't think it jess right to do such there

She knew rich folks' secrets from all over town
When their lies would arise she'd just shoot 'em down

She knew who shot the La-La and who killa the chief
and who snatched the fruit from the mispileaf

St. Louis No. 1 is where she now sleeps
But they say from the grave her soul often creeps

So when folks in New Orleans tell of those long ago
they whisper the wooing legend of Marie Laveau...

Sunday, August 19, 2012 10:47 PM
Stamford, CT

My Father's Legacy

a meager, empty metal box
a buncha dead batteries
some used fuses
and some keys that didn't fit
a muthafuckin' thing…

1999 (Revised 2008)

Fake

-went into a record store
(if they're still called dat)
and asked if there were any
Hugh Masekela
in stock...

and the dreadlocked salesperson
with the "I LOVE AFRICA" T-shirt
and the
red-black-green beads 'round his neck
didn't know
who I was
talkin'
'bout...

Wednesday, June 27, 2012

Motto

(to Langston Hughes)

If you can dig it
   you can dig it
If you cain't
   you cain't...

'cuz if you with it
   you is with it

If you ain't

   you ain't...

July 2012
Stamford, CT

Glass Flowers

(to Rosa Colón)

Glass Flowers...
Impassioned petals, blooming blossoms
purely painted, mirrored reflections
blendings of spirit essence, motion, lust, love and life
eternal truths from hallowed hands
a heaving heart
blistering-hot breath in dens dark and dangerous
sophisticated soothings and cooly-scented smells
wings and singing things
saintly sonatas, eversprouting skyward
dreams, undeferred
no bullet wounds or razor cuts
no beer bottles or broken noses
no high, no low
no rejections
just introspection's resurrections...

Glass flowers...
passionate paeans from unpursed lips
exquisite, finespun fun
in coldness of winter or hot Southern sun
Softness and beauty
so far above duty...

Glass flowers (just like life)
-all they're cracked up to be...

Sunday, November 13, 2011   5:39 PM
Stamford, CT

To a Temptress

I've done my share of wrong in life
but I've never laid down with another man's wife...
You've been with him now for decades long
in bitingly bitter cold and soft summersong
Your lips are enticing
your sweetness, such icing
your laughter, seductive
your words, so instructive...
But I don't do evil so willingly
and cannot love so illicitly
or consign my feelings freely
to one with a heart so steely
to break a vow so quickly
in a dalliance so sickly...
I ain't never laid down with another man's wife
in this earthbound realm (or in any other life)
I'd rather be alone and lonesome
for doing so would be loathsome
and though a lust for you might linger
a ring sits sparkling on your finger
If you treat such troth like forsaken debris
what lowdown evil might you do to me?

Saturday, February 9, 2013 8:06 AM
Stamford, CT

Relationship Therapy

I Don't Love You Anymore (Poem # 101)

I don't love you anymore
I don't love you anymore
I don't love you anymore
I don't love you
I don't love you
I don't love you
I don't love
I don't love
I don't love
I don't
I don't
I don't...

Tuesday, November 25, 2008 5:42 AM
Stamford, CT

Rationality (Poem # 103)

I loved her yesterday, today
and all of our tomorrows…
and will do so
forever…
but I know
that one day
her soft, smooth skin
will shrivel like a fallen leaf
in the hot, summer sun
her heavensent, inviting breasts
will become as parched as the desert sands
her sweetness will sour
and the irresistible magnets that are her eyes
will see only the dust and darkness of the grave
but
the earth that my heart becomes
will perpetually drumbeat
a ceaseless song
of my boundless, everlasting, eternal love for her
forever…

Monday, July 25, 2011 4:35 PM
Stamford, CT

Reality (Poem # 104)

You read GLAMOUR
I read AARP
(You say) you're ready to get married

I'm ready to croak...

Monday, July 25, 2011 4:45 PM
Stamford, CT

Lady in the Picture (Poem # 105)

The irresistible magnets that are your eyes
sing a majestic presence bringing strength and fulfillment
I can't remove your scent from memory
or erase your lipstick on the poem you gave me
At least one moment of each day
I surrender to your splendor
for there's nothing one can do to make me stop loving you
At that one moment each day
my heart is made stronger
as we make aural love
(reading your poems over and over and over)
over time, uneternal
as I gaze in the stillness and quiet of the room
under those irresistible magnets
that are your eyes...

Tuesday, September 27, 2011 4:56 AM
Stamford, CT

Illumination

The sun screams its fire alive
as I offer this melody of words in homage to her
and again sing her morningsong...
of the bounty of her beauty (its sanctity and lust)
of her hypnotic allure
of her quietness and strength
of the truth she speaks in whispered prayer
of her departure with a smile on her silksoft lips...
Each morning I thank God for her blessings and being
and pray that the devil send forth his champions
(the worldly unwise who speak with tongues of tarnished silver)
I pray they come forward so I might slay them with my words
for her beauty dispatches the wicked and brings light from the shadows
Although the long-coveted landscape of her flesh is distant and removed
she yet breathes her passion through the night
and I feel the beauteous rendition of her hot hauntings in the day...
She is the loveliest flower in all the world's gardens
(engaging and enchanting)
I am but a mortal being in this waning flesh
I eat, sleep, pray and sin in this realm of disillusionment and despair
but the spirit of the Lord often animates and enlivens my heart
and I take refuge in the sublime treasure of her remembrance
for she is woman (the source of all creation)
forever inspiring and blacknificent...
The life I chose can be lonely indeed
but I swim in the seas of her satisfaction...
The forever temple of her beauty
can be on the farthest side of the world
but infinity itself cannot abate the ultimate joy and refreshment
of this morningsong reaching heavenward
that sings of the spirit of salvation and peace
even her absence bestows on my being...

Monday, June 10, 2013 7:10 AM
Stamford, CT

Morning

Again I am in awe at the uniqueness of your sweetness
 as the echoes of our last loving soar through the skies...
Inharmonious humans mutter and sputter
 trampling and trudging to their dull-as-dishwater duties
The day blooms so dramatically ecstatically erratically
The symmetry of your lips, the tantalizing textures of your hips
 beckon to my epicurean cravings from a continent away...
Yet do I marvel at the uniqueness of your exquisiteness
Every day with you is a honeymoon
Without you, life is perpetual dissolution
Our yesterday dreams envelop all that is us
My destiny is to dwell forever in your otherworldly magic
Transcendental truths are baptized in your words
 and confirmed in creation's caress...
Your embodiment sings a morning melody
The breath of life that is you inspires desire's fires in me...
The song of David forevermore sears my soul
 for I'll never love another (after loving you)
I'll never write another love poem (if not about you)
I never wish to see another sunrisen morning
 if the earth's shining, simmering star ever outrivals the artistry
 of your allure...
My life's most gratifying commission
 is to chronicle the measure of your resplendence
 and I genuflect in supplication and welcome such delicately
 delightful endeavor...

Tuesday, April 22, 2014 6:32 AM
Stamford, CT

42

Shikorina*

You inspire desire in my soul's deepest substance
I am fascinated by God's enchanting artistry
You are 13 months of sunshine
and immeasureable shades of immaculateness...
That is who you are
This is who I am
This is what God is and will forever and ever be
for He has been good to me
He saved me from myself
He extended His grace when I slipped and tripped
in the world's dim, dark shadows
We know not of our future (but dwell within its grasp)
Forever waters flow
past the time-ravished bellicose and belligerent
past the bearers of unprofound burdens and tellers of tall tales
past legions of dark-eyed beauties
with lips like copper and breasts like satin...
You are in my life for however long you choose to be
Your unrivaled sweetness is legendary
Your kindness and pleasantness are eternal blessing
Seeing a mere glimpse of your shadow is uplifting
Your harmonious melodies sing the truths of God's messengers
I know not of a promise of tomorrow
for that promise is not guaranteed to any mortal
Only God can assure the fortunate
of an enduring knowledge of your comeliness
Only God can construct a being of such fathomless expanses
whose relishing taste is more than mere fantasy by a poet
on this place
called
Earth...

Sunday, September 22, 2013 9:10 AM
Stamford, CT

sweet like sugar

SCREAM

I scream the passion and pleasures of this life
-the love, admiration and adulation I have for my beloved, my distant lover
I scream it publicly and without reservation, for she is my eternally beloved
I scream as I stand in the evening's light, contemplating her beauty
I scream for God's Oneness
I scream for God's mercy
I scream for the believers
I scream for her softness and soul
for God reveals His truth
in His own time
in His own way...
I scream a song of life and fulfillment
1 scream of the traditions God has revealed
I scream of the poetry I sing of her in the shower
for God wills it so in His own way...
I scream of a life filled with happiness
(and sometimes with strife)
I scream of not merely lying next to her
(for such lying is indeed not truth)
I scream for the beauty of her land as reflected in her hands
I scream for the hapless and hopeless unhappenings
the instruments of love and war
for the pain and strife of this mortal life...
for her unrivaled beauty and profundity of thought...
I chase the shadows of her music, laughter and prayer
through the generosity of the goddess of nature
and the soundless room
of our talk this evening
and our fusion in these mortal days...
God is indeed great
for I am surely blessed
through knowing the essence of her beatific flesh
in this soundless room
as inspired by the eternal rhythm of her sumptuous screams...

Tuesday, July 30, 2013 6:49 PM
Stamford, CT

44

ASTER

You reveal a glorious destiny
(ecstatic ecstasy)
In your eyes are endlessly eternal starlit skies
    in your walk, an Amharic love song...
Your beauty is a debt paid forthwith
The fragrances that surround you are inspiring
I write of your allure not to those now living
    but to those who will enter the sphere of this existence
    at some time in the future...
The enchantment in your eyes is a thrilling stimulation
Your beauty purges my being of all wrath and anger
God is reflected in your majesty
I marvel at His radiant creation
You, daughter of Africa, are the manifestation of His greatest work
Your smile is happiness and glory
The Lord's eminence is reflected in the secret gardens of your
fleshly delights
    as He makes His magic through these unpretentious words...
Your character and demeanor are indeed stunning
The woman in you radiates for all eternity
The Godliness and virtue in you speaks volumes
Your kindliness, devoutness and goodness radiate honesty and truth
I revel in the thought of knowing you
    for that knowledge is fundamental to my comprehension of the
world
I thank God for the awareness of you and your hallowed presence
    for you are the greatest reward of existence in this diminished
journey
    that we unremarkable humans
    call life...

Saturday, August 31, 2013 7:08 PM
Stamford, CT

Fragrance

Last night,
    you told me I should write more about God...
I, therefore, seek His guidance and inspiration
    to write of His radiant creation
    for every day with you is a holiday (and a holy day)
    under skies that God garnished with an ocean of stars...
The arousing aroma of your beauty's bouquet
evinces the latest rebeginning of our forever love affair
Your magical fires, the perfumes of desire
    awaken me from maddening nightmares in memory's mirror
    and recollections of the irreverent and irrelevant
    with no rhyme for their reasons and gold, their only god...
I give you my heart and soul (again)
    the fervor of my fidelity (again)
    the music and melody of these words (again)
I sense your prayers rising heavenward
    from your firelike lips and angelic endearments...
My heart belongs to no other (and I've never truly loved anyone but you)
My eyes are filled with tears at the thought of your absence
Your preeminence is astounding
    for the Divine Being brought you
        the All Powerful taught you
The joy of your loving laughter, your sighs
    are forever delectable and delightful
Your name forever echoes throughout the highest of heavens
    by dint of this poet's humble words
    for those unblessed with the awareness and comprehension
    of encountering the aromatic potion of such splendid creation...

Sunday, September 15, 2013 10:35 AM
Stamford, CT

46

I Miss You

I miss you
I miss your kisses and caresses
  and your constant prayer that blesses…
I miss the music of your muse
I miss your laughter in bright, moonlight night
I miss your eyes
I miss your lips
I miss your sweet, sugarsoft hips
I miss your voice
I miss your accent
I miss the robe you wear
I miss watching you braid your hair
I miss the sparkle of your eyes
  the truths that you surmise…
I miss the sweat of our lovemaking through the night
  and serving you breakfast in bed in the morning…
I miss your sharing of your secrets
I miss your whispers
I miss your constant talking
I miss your constant talking
I miss your constant talking
I miss watching you applying your lipstick
  and spraying your perfume…
I miss our late night talks and long, wisdom walks
I miss your laughter
I miss the incense and herb of your merriment
I miss our romancing and dancing
(I miss your takin' me to the next phase, baby)
I miss yo' lovin' and yo' cookin' (good-lookin')
I miss your sleek, silky things lying on the bedpost
I miss chasing you around the room (Come git wit daddy, baby)
I miss contemplating the stars with you on the balcony

I miss our prolonged discussions about old times and newer futures
I miss your misinterpretations
I miss the ceaseless pleasures of your innermost treasures
LAWD, have mercy, mercy, mercy
I miss you...
you...

Sunday, March 9, 2014 12:01 AM
Stamford, CT

Melody

The winds of love blow where they wish
    and my heart and hand sing once again of your beauty
    for the melody of your muse is intoxicating
Love roots spread jubilance in the garden of your warmth
The passion of your merriment is sunset's song
Your laughter is the envy of the ages
Mother Jazz made you a symphony of prayer and indulgence
Father God blessed me with the knowledge of you
Our love has made us co-authors of our own dreams
My deep sense of you is intimate and infinite
You are my lifetime lover and I, your perpetual paramour
You strengthen me when I am fearful as I watch you at worship
You teach me how to love again...
The memory of your moistness haunts my meditations
    in this cold land where women wear dead people's hair
    and I dwell in this pitiful parade among the ratchet of the earth
My time in this world's wilderness is made meaningful by our intimacies
    for this might be the last time in life that I have the opportunity to love
    someone who truly loves me...
I can't waste that time...
    for there is no life or living without your loving...
If the last time I saw you is the last time I'll ever see you
    the flame of our passion will be here still...
When I perish and my flesh is rotted and putrid
    our love will forever be retained and recollected
      in the hallowed, haunting melody of these words...

Saturday, April 12, 2014 8:25 PM
Stamford, CT

Mosaic

A mosaic of emotion gushes forth
as I write of the rapture of her enticing elegance
and the constancy of this amorous adventure in the seas of satisfaction...
This sometime bitter, lonely, often nightmarish life I chose
can be eerily silent
but she again makes known a morsel of paradise...
Although my destiny is to not have a household
filled with children's laughter
and my vulnerabilities and weaknesses might flourish
I carve this monument to the memory of her...
for the constellation of her life force
for the many different ways she loves
for the promise of her pleasures
for her touch
for her cuddles and cravings...
I write in this unassuming place with pen, paper and her prayers...
Heaven is in her sentiment
Heaven is in her radiance
Heaven is in her morning prayers
Heaven is in the sweetness of her refrain
Heaven is in the promise of her pleasures...
I write amidst the presence of this remarkable mortal
as she communes with God in this place
and strive to portray her image
for those future generations of those less fortunate souls yet unborn
whose field of vision will never behold
the brilliant flame of her enduring beauty...

Friday, January 4, 2013 6:35 AM
Stamford, CT

Guidance

I cannot resist the undeniable awesomeness of your embrace
    for the profundity of change is mirrored in your semblance
I will never carry a stone in my heart towards you
    for the spirit guides my hand to neither condemn nor judge...
The preeminence of your thoughts blends blissfully with morning air
Forever is your flavor when fate extends its fickle hand
Depression and disillusionment are perished
The clarity of your guidance has revealed the accursed and the blessed
The past, though buried, only sleeps in this quiet room
Memory is glacially frozen in place
Last night I awoke, bellicose and belligerent, sweating and screaming
    but your everlasting profundity salvaged my sanity
I believe in your rendering of strength to weakness
I believe in the fortune in your meaningfulness
I believe in your capacity for compassion...
You are a fount of encouragement pouring uninterrupted sageness
You are the pathfinder to inexhaustible enticement
Your fervency is the flame of intensity
Fear is faded and forgotten, torment long departed
The corrupt and malicious are cast aside, shunned by your supplication
Sustenance is evident in your goodness and calmness
The pleasures of your panting indulge my hungers
The floodgates of your streamlet are unbolted as I dauntlessly enter the
    heavens inside the bliss of your enchantment
Yours is the abode of the blessed
Encircling you is the firmament of a forever treasure...

Thursday, January 3, 2013 6:01 AM
Stamford, CT

Aspiration

The air around you is perfumed with the sensual and spiritual
Gulls glide over the frosted channel
    as the sun simmers far above its glimmering glaze...
Your morning recitations make evil seem lifeless
    for you are one of His anointed children
    (antithesis to the colorblindness of wickedness)
Your interblending with the spirit is ascendant enterprise
The entwinement of your embrace is inescapable
The loftiness of your thoughts, ineludible...
You are foreordained to again awake
    and consecrate the world with your radiance...
You reflect the living Word and the Word resounds all that is you
I aspire to effect this portrait of your comeliness
    remote from the city's clamor far below...
The land's faithful walk in the Word
The symmetry of your brilliancy emanates from the Word
The entrance to your tantalizing tideway resides in your image
It surpasses all that is known and unknown
I endeavor to discover the most secret of your parts
    and explore them with no reluctance or pretension...
Hesitation is unperceived; satisfaction, pleasant disclosure
I know not from whence you came, nor question your origins
    for I have faith that one so savory
    could only have been begotten
    from the most sequestered, holy place
    in the vastness of all creation...

Wednesday, January 2, 2013 8:19 AM
Stamford, CT

Mysterioso

Father,

Grant me the grace to bid You greetings this morning
    and the strength to burst into song in homage to Your perfection...
for my beloved mirrors the artistry of Your masterstroke of conception
Her likeness replicates the mystery of our journey in the carnival of life...
I believe in Your creations, so wide and wonderful
The communion I feel with Your eternal skyscape is awe-inspiring
My consciousness arises and I am mindful of Your power
    as I reach for her light in the darkness...
You are made manifest in the communion of our merging
Your Word is made flesh in the poetry of our intensity
The unbending magic of your mercy divulges unhindered tidings
    of our temporal beginning and transformation to the celestial...
Your truth resonates the air, water and fires of our journey
Although I am but flesh and blood, Your guardian spirit
    speaks with grandiloquent precision
I am disconcerted and stunned by the inception of these words
    but trust that You guide my hand in embodying Your grandeur
    in this effortless portrait of Your preeminent work...
For it is within woman that we reside until we emerge into the world
Within woman, all saints have come
Within woman, the mystery of all creation is anchored...
I pray that You continue to endow me with mortal life
if only to capture the amazement of our dawning
through these humble words as I attempt to portray the depths and mystery
of this now-breathing spirit
lying next to me

in the darkness...

Sunday, December 30, 2012 6:22 AM
Stamford, CT

53

Secret Garden

The Healer speaks through your outpourings of compassion
You have again awakened adventure's sensations
Your lushness reflects God's ripening of the seed of inspiration
inside my self...
His unrestricted resourcefulness has aroused the intensity of my craving
        to again give birth to a picture of your delectable countenance...
I do not grow weary of writing about your beauty
        for its muse is unsurpassable arousal...
The progression of your flowering and uniqueness is perpetual
        as you teach me to live in the light of the Lord...
Your supplications undo the latest wrong I have done
The eternal life force is celebrated in your sentiments
All praises are due your prayers
All praises are due your fount of inspiration
All praises are due your touch
All praises are due your aroma
All praises are due your heat
All praises are due your enduring pulsations
All praises are due the unseen angels of your transcendence...
I am mere scribe of this newer testament to you
but The Healer speaks through my soul of your wonders
and the fluidity of these words of adulation ascend heavenward
for The Great One's glory indeed resides in you
as we dance again to the harmonious magic and splendor of His creations
Outside, a nightchill still lingers
but there is only warmth and endearment in this pitiful attempt
to capture the aura of the secret garden
comprising the choicest of blossoms
that is my relentless, unremitting love...

Thursday, December 27, 2012 6:21 AM
Stamford, CT

Addis Ababa

Addis Ababa means "new flower"
and there is no flower more delicately dazzling than you
Your unrivaled loveliness is the envy of all nature
You ignite my intellect and compassion
in a strange, otherworldly fashion
Each morning when you are asleep or at prayer
I write a melody to your epic refrain
While you are talking to God
I set forth the splendor of His creation
for God dwells within you...
You are His most wondrous conception
God is all around you
for His mercy and beneficence are reflected in your mortal substance
God is everywhere...
God is in your touch
God is in the melody of your whispers
God is in your eyes
and the pleasure in your sighs
God is in your prayers, flowing skyward
God is in your laughter
here and ever after...
God is in your silences
God is in the way you massage my aging flesh
God is in my pledge to you to write a thousand poems
in praise of your being
for your aromatic song must be rendered and sung
for the joyfulness and bliss
of those of us yet unborn...

Sunday, December 23, 2012 2:10 AM
Stamford, CT

Habibti*

The sacred space of our loving
is saddened by your absence
The walls cry out
for your exotic, hypnotic, erotic presence
The memory of the emerald green of your Red Sea eyes
no longer blesses the innards of our coupling
but your smile is everpresent…
I hear your voice in the silence
smell your perfume through the sheets
feel your wetness in the air
sense your prayers…
You will soon be in my arms again
and I, enshrouded in your warmth
There is no sadness in your absence
for your mirth rejoices, shouting from the heavens
God is in your remembrance
I hear your litany of entreaties to the Grand Designer
Who granted me your pleasures
Who hears your imploring
Who is reflected in our love
Who has returned my beloved
to my embrace
for an infinity of loving
that will last
far beyond the ages…

Thursday, December 20, 2012 8:25 AM
Stamford, CT

*my beloved

Lost and Found

Found Poem

Lies Men Tell Women:

I ain't been with a woman in a while.
I had a vasectomy.
I'ma just put the head in.
I won't cum in your mouth.
We broke up.
OOH!!! This is the best posse I ever had.
We gon' git engaged.
I live alone.
I'm single.
I'd like to take you to my place, but my momma staying with me
    'til she get better.
I don't wanna have SEX with you...I wanna make LOVE to you, baby.
That's my niece's number on the cell.
I'ma give that back to you on payday.
That love poem I wrote was about you.
She's too young for me.
My cell is about to die.
That's my sister. She came over to cook for me tonight.
I would've been home last night, but I had a flat and my spare was flat too.
I'm on my way. I'm walking out the door.
I'ma be right back. I gotta get something outa my car.
She's just a friend.
I'ma call you right back.
I never married her. We were just living together.
Can you drive? My car is in the shop.
I'm only gon' use your car about an hour.
I'ma spend Valentine's Day with my momma.
Let me see a lil' bit, just a lil' bit...
Me and the fellas was just out talking and playing cards.
Everybody got a lap dance but me.
No baby, I wasn't staring at her; she looks like my cousin.
I love you.

Lies Women Tell Men:

Yes, I come every time.
Yeah, baby. It was goo-oo-oo-ood.
You're the best I've ever had.
Ooh baby! You're the BIGGEST I've ever had!
I'm cumming!!! I'm cumming!!! (sound effect and sigh)
All those muscles may be OK for some women, but I prefer you, boo.
My daddy's taking me out for dinner on my birthday.
God knows I love you.
I can't talk long, because I don't have a lot of minutes left on my cell.
He's my roommate.
I'm in a meeting.
We can still be friends.
He's too old for me.
I'll be there in a minute....
I've never done anything like this before.
It's not you, baby. It's me.
I'm not upset.
I never felt like this before.
I don't want you for your money.
We'll go "dutch."
He's just a friend.
Sugar daddy? That's my uncle you saw me with.
I'm not trying to marry you.
I'm gonna marry you one day.
I put something in the mail for you.
I'm celibate.
I'm on the pill.
I was out with the girls.
I haven't spoken to my ex in ages.
I love you.

Thursday, October 2, 2014 4:53 AM
Stamford, CT

Hate Speech

"You don't value my opinion."
"You think too much of yourself."
"You have low self-esteem."
"We never talk."
"That's all you do is talk."
"That's why we can't have children."
"You never wanted children."
"You don't love me anymore."
"Stop trying to love me so much."
"You haven't bought me anything lately."
"You're always trying to buy my love."
"You're too possessive."
"You don't pay enough attention to me."
"You joke too much."
"You're too serious."
"You're getting old."
"You're so immature."
"Why can't you have another drink with me?"
"You drink too much."
"You're too quiet."
"You're too loud."
"You never consider my point-of-view."
"You can't think for yourself."
"You're too weak."
"You're so overbearing."
"Can you lower your voice?"
"Can you speak louder?"
"You're calling a bit early."
"You're calling too late."
"You never call me from work."
"You call me too much from work."
"I hate you."
"I wish you were the one Georgie shot."

Thursday, June 19, 2014   2:33 PM
Stamford, CT

The Man Rules

Never trust a woman
Never send a boy to do a man's job
Never put the pussy on a pedestal
Never rob a bail bondsman
Never bring a knife to a gunfight
Thou shalt not covet thy neighbor's wife ('specially when her husband
    is an insanely jealous gun enthusiast with a fifth-degree black belt)
Never block a beer truck
Don't buy the cow if you can get the milk for free
Never give a woman more than you can afford for her to leave you with
Never hit on the help
Never fornicate with the help
Every crowd has a fool: never be the fool in the crowd
Never try to play a player
Never try to bullshit a bullshitter
Never let your left hand know what your right hand is doing (it might ge
    jealous)
Always fry chicken with a shirt on
Don't let your lil' head rule your big head
Treat a hoe like a lady and a lady like a hoe
A hard dick has no conscience
Don't drop a load where you eat
Never tell a woman when payday is
Don't marry "fine"…marry "thin" (if you feel you must)
Everything that looks good *ain't* good
Don't try to make a hoe a housewife
Never cry in public (even at yo' own momma' funeral)
Never hit on your podner's oldlady
Never drink the last beer
Never bring a broad to the battle
Never lead with your dick
If you cain't get the whole dog—don't take the turd
Never drink and drive (Pull over and finish the bottle)
Never go in a lady's purse
Always look in a *hoe's* purse
Never speak for another man's rod

Never trust a pussy (cuz a pussy's a lyin' set o' lips)
Never let a woman "give" you your freedom—and never let one take it
 away
Never foam up the beer
Never call a bitch a hoe
Never call a hoe a bitch
Mind your own business
Never get your honey where you make your money
Never get your cream where you make your bread
Never lend nobody your car, your gun or your dick
Always obey the "I buy...you fly" rule
Never try to rob a gun store
Always get the pussy where you find it
Leave a hoe where you find a hoe
Never admit guilt
Never admit anything
Never admit that you were wrong
Don't admit—*accuse*
There's no such thing as too much money, titty, pussy, ass or beer
Always call a woman "Baby" when you hittin' it (You'll never slip up and
 say the wrong name)
Never believe nuthin' a woman says
Never come where you shouldn't go
Never put cologne on your nuts (*Ouch!*)
Never...ever...Never...ever...NEVER walk down the aisle....

Thursday, August 8, 2013   7:33 PM
Stamford, CT

The Liar

"I love you"

(she said)

as his

cum

trickled

down

her

thigh...

Arthur Pfister
Circa 1978 (Revised 2009)

I'm a Hater

(to all the haters in the house)

Yeah…
I'm a hater
I hate when people use the word "hater"
I hate havin' to get up early to go to work
I hate runnin' outa beer
I hate Sunday "blue laws"
I hate $20 lap dances
I hate prophylactics that break
I hate people who call rubbers "prophylactics"
I hate designer clothes (I ain't no walkin' billboard)
I hate people who cherrypick their sins
I hate cafeteria Christians who choose their transgressions
    from immoral menus
I hate havin' herb (and no rollin' papers)
I hate havin' rollin' papers (and no herb)
I hate not havin' no lighter when I *got* the papers *and* the herb
    (and I *really* hate not havin' 'nair one)
I hate poems that's too short (if there is such a thing)
I hate poems that's too long (if there is such a thing)
I hate wimmins that's too pretty (if there is such a thing)
I hate wimmins that's too fine (if there is such a thing)
I hate pussy that's too good (if there is such a thing)
I hate titties that's too titillating (if there is such a thing)
I hate havin' too much money and too much honey (if there
    is such a thing)
I hate people who don't like the Three Stooges and cowboy movies
I hate people who talk about their "ancestors" when they
    don't even know they paw
I hate people who ask poets to do free gigs when they have budgets
    (*we* gotta eat too)
I hate so-called poets who think Amiri Baraka is a character
    in *Mortal Kombat*
I hate when poets use clichés like "my Nubian Ki-i-iing…
    my Nubian Quee-ee-een"
I hate sour cream on tacos (I don't eat nuthin' sour—
    I just eat sweet thangs)

I hate people who spend $100 on a concert ticket, but cain't pay $5
    for the Spoken Word set
I'm a hater…
I hate people who call you a hater
I hate people who say "playa hater"
I hate people who use the phrase "but I digress"
I hate people who use the cinematically-generated phrase
    "keepin' it real"
I hate people who use the corporately-generated slogan "real talk"
I hate radio stations that claim to be 'bout community but have
    playlists using the very gobbidge and filth doing so much damage
    to the consciousness of the people
I hate characters in movies where they see someone flying through
    the air after an explosion and they yell "*No-O-O-O-o-o-o-o-o-o-o-o-o…*"
I hate lil' white lies (and BIG BLACK LIES)
I hate CD packaging that scratches the disc when you open it
    (keep it simple, stupid)
I hate people who have tag sales—with department store prices
I hate people in public places who share their conversation
    (with the who-o-o-ole world)
I hate people who use the word "hater" (cuz I'm a hater)
I hate people who wait 'til they get on the bus—*then* begin gittin'
    their fare together
I hate seein' Christmas trees in the gobbidge
I hate people who call every person of Latino descent a "Mexican"
I hate New Orleans restaurants that ain't in New Orleans
I hate people who move to the French Quarter – and wanna ban live music
I hate people who call tourists "visitors"
I hate people who call chitlins "chitterlings"
I hate people who call milleton "merliton" (when they been callin' it
    "milleton" all along)
I hate people who drop by the crib and assume they can recharge
    their phones without asking
I hate people who borrow your food containers and (ahem)
    forget to return them

I hate people who are so cheap that they complain about people
    not returning their food containers
I hate people who talk about "the good-old days"
    (but ignore segregation)
I hate people who never had to buy their drinks "out the wall"
        never used a separate water fountain
        never sat behind the sign in the backa the bus
        never attended segregated schools
        -and think they have a clearer perspective than me on
          race relations
    (they ain't thinkin')
I hate people who have their own opinions and make them their
own facts
    (they ain't thinkin')
I hate people who think there's such a thing as a "post-racial society"
    (they ain't thinkin')
I hate people who think whoever's in the White House gon' really
make a difference
    (they ain't thinkin')
I hate people who just ain't thinkin' (they ain't thinkin')
I hate politicians—*all* politicians and their lies-lies-lies
I hate government institutions that promise Paradise and deliver Hell
I hate people who don't vote (then complain)
I hate people who hate you if you didn't vote for a Democrat
I hate people who hate you if you didn't vote for a Republican
I hate people who hate you if you didn't vote
I hate people who hate you if you *did*
I hate people who call themselves "kings and queens"
    cuz Nixon, Reagan, the Bushes, and Jimmy Carter were kings
    (and queens)
I hate educational institutions with diverse student bodies and faculties
    that look like the Daughters of the Confederacy
I hate people who teach Creative Writing and don't publish anything
    (Teach by *doing*)
I hate white women (that benefited the most from Affirmative Action
    policies) who claim they're so "underrepresented in the workforce"

I hate institutions of higher education that boast of their diverse
    student populations but have only 2 out of 102 fulltime African
    American professors (like Norwalk Community College)
I hate businesses that open late and wanta rush you out the door on time
I hate gittin' ripped off
I hate high cable prices
I hate hidden fees
I hate companies that charge fees to send you a bill
I hate bank fees levied for cashing checks (written on they own bank)
I hate insurance companies that annually raise their premium "just
    because"
I hate electronic products that happen to come out just before Christmas
I hate hundred dollar tickets to see two-dollar talent
I hate entertainers who stage "wardrobe malfunctions"
I hate people who go to every Second Line in history
    but don't make it to *one* parent-teacher meeting
    (and wonder why they chirrens is treated so bad)
I hate gobbidge that passes for music
I hate cooning and buffooning by multi-millionaire artists
    (who don't *have* to be coons and buffoons)
I hate people who look at dead, bullet-riddled gangsta rappers as heroes
    rather than ministers of modern minstrelry
I hate people who say something (then repeat it)
I hate people who say something (then repeat it)
I hate people who say something (then repeat it)
I hate bands that play too loud over the poetry
I HATE POETS THAT READ TOO LOUD
I HATE POETS THAT READ TOO LOUD
I HATE POETS THAT READ TOO LOUD
I hate wimmins who want me to read to them on the phone all night
    -and don't buy 'nair book (talkin' 'bout "I like yo' voice")
I hate people who wanta treat what *they* do for *you* like business
    (but what *you* do for *them* like friendship)
I hate people who owe me and don't clear their phone's mailbox
I hate people you go find and pay back on time
    (but *you* gotta look for *them* when *they* owe *you*)

I hate photographers at poetry readings who take pitchas of me –
    and don't send me a copy (present company excepted)
I hate people who collect all kinda money at the door for poetry
    readings but don't give anything to the poets who're reading
    (present company excepted)
I hate people who start the gig late (when the performer arrives on time)
    (present company excepted)
I hate people who write a half-dozen poems
    (that their friends or significant others give the claps for at the readings)
    and they think they're the second coming of Nikki Giovanni...
I hate seeing plants, paintings and books in the trash
I hate poverty, war and want
I hate people who think that history started with their date of birth
    ("Dat was befo' my time...")
I hate people who started out in life on third base (and think they
    hit a home run)
I hate people with exotic-sounding African names
    (who still act like negroes)
I hate people who believe everything they're taught
I hate people who play it like they *so-o-o-o* intellectual
    (and they be just as ign'ant as me)
I hate people who refer to Malcolm as a "civil rights leader"
I hate people who confuse the Black Liberation Movement
    with the Civil Rights Movement
I hate people who fart on crowded elevators
    (and act like they didn't do it)
I hate people who think they a expert on everything imaginable
    cuz they got a Facebook page
I hate people who post duck-lipped pitchas on Facebook
I hate people on Facebook who present an illogical argument
    and you address it and they write, "That's not the point
    nor the topic of this thread."
I hate people who wax poetic about the most challenging issues of our
    (or any other) time
    –and cain't spell
I hate people who write "Have a bless day" (and leave off the 'ed')

I hate old people who think all young people are dumb
I hate young people who think all old people are dumb
I hate young people who think they hip (just cuz they young)
I hate old people who think they wise (just cuz they old)
I hate people who don't pronounce their t's
  —'Manha-in'…'Mar-in'…Hillary 'Clin-in'…'Hay-in' (No he di-in')
I hate women who wanta be a man one minute then fall back into that
  "tortured female" role the next (*"I'ma call the police…"*)
I hate women who claim they're so independent and liberated
  (but still expect the man to pay)
I hate walkin' through MACY's cosmetics department and being
  greeted by phony saleslady smiles (I don't need nuthin' here)
I hate *dumb* wimmins (and cain't *stand* they girlfriends)
I hate people who ask for J-PEGS (insteada just sayin' "pitchas")
I hate people who use abbreviations and acronyms
  (when merely typing or saying the entire word or phrase
  would suffice)
I hate when companies send me an envelope in the mail designed
  to make it look like a check is inside
I hate paintings with Malcolm, Martin and Obama
  (as though he belong in that company)
I hate people who hate "ObamaCare" but support
  the Affordable Care Act (duh-uh-uh…)
I hate people who leave the lint in the filter after dryin' they clothes
I hate people who got jobs as bank tellers
  (and front like they runnin' the Federal Reserve)
I hate doo-doo, bugars and snot
I hate people who measure their worth by what possessions they got
I hate people who measure their worth by how many Facebook pages
  they got
I hate people who see history only through their particular group's
  perspective
I hate people who condemn police violence and ignore thug violence
I hate people who condemn thug violence and ignore police violence

I hate people who think that no young, black males should be in the jails
    What about the grandma killers and the baby rapers?
    or the grandma rapers and the baby killers? (Everybody ain't Trayvon)
I hate wigs and weaves and people's pet peeves
I hate Watergate and people who constantly show up late
    (or never wanta go "Dutch" on a date)
I hate the word "hate"
and I especially, 'specially, 'specially
hate people
who write long poems
about "haters"…

Sunday, August 25, 2013 8:29 PM
Stamford, CT

Patron Saints

We (Catholics) have "Patron Saints"...
-intercessors on our behalf in obtaining benefits from God
(Jesus Christ!)
-a sacredly singular honor
-unquantifiable emotions of paraliturgical devotions
(genuflective venerations of pious generations)

The Patron Saint of *this*
The Patron Saint of *that*
The Patron Saint of kit
The Patron Saint of kat...
The Patron Saint of short
The Patron Saint of tall
The Patron Saint of you
The Patron Saint of y'all...
The Patron Saint of television is St. Clare of Assisi
The Patron Saint of fishermen (St. Andrew)
The Patron Saint of librarians (St. Jerome)
The Patron Saint of housewives (St. Anne)
The Patron Saint of missions (St. Peter Claver and St. Benedict the Black)
The Patron Saint of skiers (St. Bernard)
The Patron Saint of soldiers (St. Hadrian, St. George, St. Ignatius,
    St. Sebastian, St. Martin of Tours, St. Joan of Arc)
The Patron Saint of infantrymen (St. Maurice)
The Patron Saint of lawyers (Sts. Ivo and St. Genesius & Moore)
The Patron Saint of policemen (St. Michael)
The Patron Saint of prisoners (St. Dismas)
The Patron Saint of the falsely accused (St. Raymond Nonnatus)
The Patron Saint of poor souls (St. Nicholas of Tolentino)
The Patron Saint of sculptors (St. Claude)
The Patron Saint of rheumatism (St. James the Greater)
The Patron Saint of Bad Knees (St. Arthritis)
The Patron Saint of maids (St. Zita)
The Patron Saint of porters (St. Christopher)
The Patron Saint of priests (St. Pedophilia)
The Patron Saint of comedians (St. Vitus)

The Patron Saint of the mentally ill (St. Dymphna)
The Patron Saint of headache sufferers (St. Teresa of Avila)
The Patron Saint of tailors (St. Homobonus)
The Patron Saint of Boy Scouts (St. George)
The Patron Saint of young girls (St. Agnes)
The Patron Saint of winos (St. Willy)
The Patron Saint of crack dealers (St. Roch)
The Patron Saint of restaurants (St. Dooky)
The Patron Saint of food (St. Gumbo)
The Patron Saint of jazz (St. Trane)
The Patron Saint of New Awlins jazz (St. Satchmo)
The Patron Saint of the LAPD (St. Rodney of Kingus)
The Patron Saint of jails (St. Tulane & Broad)
The Patron Saint of bullshootin' preachers (St. Ike)
The Patron Saint of BUTT (St. Bertha)
The Patron Saint of ASS (St. Boo-ta-a-a-a-a-ay!)
The Patron Saint of Christmas (St. Nick)
The Patron Saint of con men (St. Slick)
The Patron Saint of orgies (Yo' maw)
The Patron Saint of hoes (Yo' maw again)
The Patron Saint of porno movies (Guess who?)
The Patron Saint of lips (St. Lewinsky)
The Patron Saint of Beef (St. Long Dong)
The Patron Saint of MO' Beef (Guess who again?)
The Patron Saint of war (St. George II)
The Patron Saint of mammies (St. Condoleezza)
The Patron Saint of Right Wing Conservatism (St. Limbaugh)
The Patron Saint of Dirty Tricks (St. Nixon)
The Patron Saint of embittered, losing football coaches (St. Mora)
The Patron Saint of journalistic inaccuracy (St. Picayune)
The Patron Saint of high energy bills (St. NOPSI)
The Patron Saint of Ku Klux Klansmen tryin' to front like
    they human beings (St. David of Duke)
The Patron Saint of hearts (St. Valentine)
The Patron Saint of farts (St. *Poo*-Poo)
The Patron Saint of lonely men (St. Beechameat)
The Patron Saint of lonely women (St. Vibratio)
The Patron Saint of gay men (St. Closet)
The Patron Saint of gay women (J. Edgar Hoover?!?!!!)

The Patron Saint of street niggers (St. Superfly)
The Patron Saint of lip-synchin' (St. Vanilli)
The Patron Saint of noses (St. Bugar)
The Patron Saint of *runny* noses (St. Snottious)
The Patron Saint of genital diseases (St. Vitalis)
The Patron Saint of Patron Saints (St. Patron)

Patron Saints   Aw, Patron Saints
They is what they is and they ain'ts what they ain'ts

Patron Saints   Aw, Patron Saints
Law-aw-aw-awd, how I loves them Patron Saints...

ARTURO "Professor" Pfister
Saturday, December 15, 2001

Dawn

I love the smell of poetry in the morning...
amidst the world where dwellers dwell
and buyers buy and sellers sell...
Night interblends into the past
Life's ongoing drama is now recast...
Oh!
Morning sky is so divine
in each smooth, uncluttered, florid line...
Purple passion is the vault of heaven
as watchers await the news at seven...
A runner scrambles to an early bus
Bikers bike as morning lovers thrust
Morning shadows tickle toes
Willows weep as a stirring cock crows...
Memories of last night's toasts and laughter
are now foregone forever after...
Joggers spring so swiftly by
Lovers share secrets as passions fly
Spirited squirrels scramble as a cool cat stalks
Hounds hang with humans on doggie walks
I know not what wonders this day will bring
but Dawn's inspiration is a marvelous thing...

Saturday, August 16, 2014 @ Dawn
Stamford, CT

Life

A mere moment ago
my mother's gentle hands
bathed my youthful, unspoiled flesh
in an ancient oval, porcelain tub…
Now
I find myself
'round midnight
in the moonlight and romance
of a Manhattan street corner
begging a bewitchingly beautiful ballerina
with fire engine-red lipstick
for more enchantingly exotic, erotic pleasures
from her tantalizingly tartish tongue…

Thursday, October 9, 2014 3:49 AM

Imperfect English

(to Bono & the FCC)

I took my fuckin' ass
down to the fuckin' bar
got a fuckin' beer
talked to my fuckin' friends
ran into this fuckin' broad I knew
got a pack of fuckin' rubbers
fuckin' went to her fuckin' place
met her freaky fuckin' roommate
got fuckin' fucked-up
and fuckin'

    copulated...

Sunday 2/12/2006

Senior Moments

hoping that an old friend you've been trying to contact isn't dead
looking for a spatula...in the refrigerator
looking in the refrigerator for a spoon
looking for a can of peas...in the freezer
forgetting what you were looking for and staring in a drawer
    until you realize you're just standing there staring in a drawer
picking up the cell phone and thinking it's the computer mouse
confusing DVDs with BVDs
putting the William Tell Overture on your phone
buying your first bike for $35
(and discovering that the same basic bike is $350)
grabbing your toothbrush rather than your razor
accidentally brushing your teeth with Preparation H
putting something in a safe place so you can find it then forgetting
    where the safe place was
blaming those "terrible young folks" for all the evil in the world
enjoying an outing with your grandkids more than you do
    with your spouse
seeing "institutes" and "colleges" renamed as "universities"
being told you're a grouchy old man
being a grouchy old man
enjoying being a grouchy, old man
going to bed insteada going to the club
convincing yourself that pacing the floor at 3:30 in the morning
    is exercise
not panicking when a problem arises
using a store cart for your purchases when a handbasket would do
taking the elevator to the second floor
mailing holiday cards
knowing what holiday cards are
eating all the Halloween candy you want to
beginning sentences with, "Them youngsters out there nowadays..."
having pain in places where you didn't know you had places
coming to the realization that your bald spot is where you used
    to spray chemicals on your Afro
being surprised you still have hair

realizing how much time and energy you've wasted
    on Facebook arguments
asking someone to repeat what was said
purchasing a DVD collection of old TV commercials
being more concerned about your penny stocks than your cash on hand
telling a 45-year-old woman she's a fine, young thing
fussing out loud when no one's around
being mistaken for Morgan Freeman
having time for a hobby
cooking a gourmet meal…for yourself
purchasing footwear that's more comfortable than stylish
not buying a product merely because of the way it's marketed
plugging the phone charger into the TV remote
talking to yourself
knowing who Hopalong Cassidy was
being told you look like Frederick Douglass
listening to talk radio rather than Top 40
referring to contemporary radio as "Top 40"
asking yourself if people you knew who had died were really here
laughing at your own jokes
perceiving that money can't buy love (but it sure can rent it)
seeing how old your childhood friends look
realizing how old *you* look
trying to open the office door with the car door opener
hearing your former students talking about "the good-old days"
recognizing that aging is an achievement that beats the alternative
being thankful that you're still alive to write a poem
    about senior moments…

Thursday, October 16, 2014 6:32 PM
Stamford, CT

Why I Love Poetry

(A found poem from a Facebook friend)

Hi Professor Arturo,
I hope you are well. I just would like you to know the joy and fun
my 81-year-old mom is having reading "I'm So New Orleans"! She
is visiting for Thanksgiving and I gave her a copy. As I'm prepping
the Thanksgiving dinner she is laughing with a joy that I have not
seen in some time. You have truly brightened her day and gave us
something to reminisce about. Do not be surprised if you get a call
from an 81-year-old young named *******. She is now your biggest
fan. Take Care.

Wednesday, November 26, 2014   11:22 PM
Stamford, CT